Tasteful

New Interiors for
Restaurants and Cafés

gestalten

TABLE OF CONTENTS

Tasty Interiors That Look as Good as They Feel

Aiming to provide unforgettable, immersive experiences, restaurant creators are pushing the limits of interior design. From lush, flamboyant spaces to minimalist ascetic spots, these new places celebrate life in all its glory.

We don't just dine out to fill our bellies. We want to take a break, relax, and enjoy ourselves. Good design facilitates such experiences. Even though they're on our doorsteps, restaurants allow us to experience new locations and cuisines from the comfort of our neighborhoods. They are designed to transport their guests, helping us quench our wanderlust while remaining close to home. As such, in these environments, atmosphere is perhaps the most important element.

From cafés to bars, and restaurants to canteens, interior designers around the world are using color, lighting, materials, and texture to immerse us in cultures and aesthetics far from our daily lives. In some instances, the places they take us to exist; in others, they are worlds of make believe. Whatever the case, these interiors embody a limitless palette of possibilities. Informed by their clients' ambitions as well as their own singular visions, the designers responsible for these creations produce uncanny sensations in ordinary buildings. As we eat, drink, and dance, the otherworldly ambiance of these settings frequently lingers with us long after we've left.

Among the trends in these establishments, color is king. From saturated shades to neon lights, color is used to create different experiences, transition interiors from day to night, and immerse us

in a brighter, lighter world. At the Seville cocktail bar Naked and Famous (p. 28), for instance, a sequence of spaces created through color and light turns from bubblegum pink to glowing green. Elsewhere, dark tones are being used to instill a sense of drama. On the other side of the Mediterranean, the Michelin-starred Agli Amici 1887 in Udine, Italy (p. 22), boasts a new entrance lounge that resembles a mysterious all-blue "precious box," causing a sense of anticipation that captivates new arrivals. Meanwhile, back in Seville, Casaplata, a restaurant-cum-cocktail bar (p. 14), offers visitors a blank canvas of silvery gray walls that make pale-pink, green, and yellow furniture pop.

With these environments, there's an "anything goes" approach afoot. In them, maximalism is taken to the max, and lavish interiors layer it on. A case in point is Auyl in Kazakhstan (p. 124). Over its threshold, linen ribbons drape from ceilings into a highly textured space that brings together clay, stone, copper, travertine, wood, and jute. And that's not to mention the exquisite ornamentation and craftsmanship. At the Berlin trattoria Coccodrillo (p. 210), conversely, diners are transported to northern Italy in a bold burst of flamboyant red, where vintage Fiorucci posters, books, and bubble lights construct a fun yet refined look. On the other end of the spectrum, restaurateurs are still craving calm minimalist interiors—but with a twist. Subtly packed with features, these pared-back designs secretly incorporate hints of maximalism. At Istetyka in Kyiv (p. 136), for example, designer Victoria Yakusha has employed her sensual and emotional "live minimalism" through contrasting, serene materials. Similarly, there's also the tranquil, buttery interior of Banacado in Stockholm (p. 46), a dreamy café where pale-yellow hues conjure a sunny, cinematic sweetness.

Moreover, when these establishments aren't transporting us elsewhere, they're making us feel like we're encountering something absolutely out of this world. Employing a unique approach to greenhouse design, Äng in Halland, Sweden (p. 156), takes diners on a culinary journey through an all-glass space, which consequently shifts moods depending on the time of day. On the other hand, at Under in Norway, visitors are literally invited to eat under the sea. "Under will offer you new perspectives and ways of seeing the world," says architect Kjetil Trædal Thorsen of Europe's first underwater restaurant.

Affinities with nature are growing even stronger in today's interiors too. While biophilia itself might be de rigueur, the inclusion of greenery into design is becoming more common. In Goa, Terttúlia, a restaurant resplendent in mint and ivy (p. 242), is surrounded by coconut trees, planters, and petal lights with shades inspired by falling leaves. And at Lulu's at the Lodge in the hills of Jamberoo in Australia (p. 196), guests can drink champagne among the pines and marvel at the majestic landscape.

Connections with nature also factor in the turn to sustainable design. Rather than being crafted from scratch, today, restaurants are being carved out of existing spaces and designers are reusing materials. Set inside a former theater and recording space in Madrid, Mo de Movimiento (p. 94) is one such space. Conceived by designer Lucas Muñoz, its wooden elements have been transformed into restaurant furniture. Construction debris and reused textiles were also recycled to create benches, cushions, and kitchen tiles, as well as acoustic panels for the ceiling, where large hanging terracotta jugs offer an innovative cooling system.

In some corners, a return to retro styles is taking shape. One such establishment serving this look is Caffettiera in Montreal (p. 66), which offers an authentic slice of 1990s Italian coffee culture. Here, 20th-century collectibles are complemented by posters of supermodels and turn-of-the-century Italian soccer stars. On the other side of the globe, Blacksmith Provedore next to Lake Mulwala in New South Wales, Australia (p. 250), is reviving the Swinging Sixties through delicate furnishings and vintage flourishes. Further afield, other establishments are being seduced by visions of tomorrow. Exemplifying this is FoodX in Warsaw, Poland (p. 32), where rough, monochromatic walls host neon screens, producing a futuristic dreamscape effect.

What follows in *Tasteful*'s pages, then, is a curated selection of restaurants, cafés, bars, and canteens where the interiors are as alluring as the menus. Featuring a variety of styles from a host of different locations around the globe, this book serves as both a guide for intrepid foodies as well as inspiration for those passionate about design. From calm to colorful, cinematic to phantasmagoric, these surprising, innovative, and unconventional interiors aren't just spaces to eat or drink in, but figurative tickets to ride.

GRT Architects' design of the Alba Accanto cocktail bar
in New York features a striped fabric ceiling, built-in
bench seating, polished stone, and bright colors that reflect
the vibrance of Italian coastal cities like Positano.

Rich Colors and Rough Finishes Furnish a Roman Bar-Restaurant

TRE DE TUTTO
ROME, ITALY
STUDIOTAMAT

Created partially in tribute to the 1920s architecture of the surrounding Garbatella neighborhood, the Roman bar-restaurant Tre de Tutto combines classic modern design with rich pops of color. "Owners Mirko Tommasi and Daniele Notte offer revisited classics of Roman cuisine, taking inspiration from one of the most authentic neighborhoods in Rome," says Matteo Soddu, cofounder of Studiotamat, the atelier responsible for Tre de Tutto's design. "In the same way, our goal from the beginning was not to distort the preexisting space but to enhance it and, at the same time, bond with its clientele." Spread across two levels, the restaurant's refined yet playful interior is set inside a local bakery that had long been abandoned. On the ground floor, where three custom-designed arched windows bring generous light into the space, walls are clad in blue tiles up to waist height, while above they are left rough and untreated "to exhibit the passage of time," as Soddu notes. Recycled iron chairs in yellow and flesh pink stand out against the blue tiles, as does the doorframe to the salmon-colored staircase-tunnel leading to the lower level. Here, light-blue walls contrast with grid wallpaper featuring subtly colored geometric shapes. Further on, a bright-yellow ramp bordered by perforated sheet metal panels offers an alternative street-level entrance, giving each and every guest a warm welcome.

Light-blue walls alternate with grid
wallpaper by Texturae. Recycled iron
chairs in yellow and flesh pink complement
the color of the leather benches.

A dynamic palette was designed
to contrast with the neutral
shades of the original walls, which
were left in their original state.

A Silver-Gray Still Life That Beautifully Balances Opposites

CASAPLATA
SEVILLE, SPAIN
LUCAS Y HERNÁNDEZ-GIL / KRESTA DESIGN

Once a 1990s cafeteria, the building that Seville's Casaplata calls home has since been transformed by Madrid studio Lucas y Hernández-Gil into a contemporary cocktail bar and restaurant where delicate meets industrial. For example, furniture made of perforated metal sheets in colors like pale rose pink and blue stand out against a steelish backdrop. In all, it creates the impression of a fleeting, beautiful haze that could slip away in the blink of an eye, like a daydream. Unlike some adaptive reuse projects, Lucas y Hernández-Gil looked both forward and back when coming up with their striking, singular design for Casaplata. While taking into consideration the impact of their work on future generations, one source of inspiration was the work of the Italian modernist painter Giorgio Morandi, especially his ethereal spaces and still lifes. According to the atelier, the aim was to create a place that blurred "the lines of the environment to focus on what is within reach." The fruit of these efforts is a balance of opposites. In one corner you might find colorful, velvet seats sitting on untreated cement; in another, the silver fluted ceiling contrasts with the smooth matte finish of the floors and walls. And then there are the circular forms of a mirror, a cutout in the wall, and an inverted, floating light above the round, pale-pink centerpiece table, which contrast with the room's otherwise rigid geometry. The addition of a light-rose pigment to the plaster also gives the walls a soft silvery-gray tone, brightening the space. But at night, floating LED fixtures transform everything, turning Casaplata's industrial aesthetic into a nocturnal production of refined pleasures.

The design team behind Casaplata,
Lucas y Hernández-Gil, describes the Sevillian
cocktail bar / restaurant's contrasting
elements as "delicate meets raw."

A Retro-Futuristic Parisian Café with Bold, Dreamlike Colors

CAFÉ NUANCES
PARIS, FRANCE
UCHRONIA

At Café Nuances in Paris's eighth arrondissement, it's the color that compels. The third of the café chain's franchises in the city to be designed by French architecture firm Uchronia, its pristine white facade makes the vivid color inside stand out. Painted on floors and walls, the coffee shop's gradient of indigo blue to orange was inspired by Uchronia founder Julien Sebban's travels to the Tunisian desert and the sunsets he witnessed there. Intended to accentuate the brand's colorful, retro-futuristic vision, it creates a dreamlike atmosphere inside. This feeling is also engendered by the fittings and furnishings, including the otherworldly shimmer of the stainless steel counter and the metal-effect cushions on the benches. Behind the counter, the space's signature orange lacquer is applied to shelves displaying the cafe's artisanal coffee, which also contributes to this fantastical mood. Reflective lava stone floor tiles also make a big impression, as do the kidney-shaped Bisou stools, which can be used as either seating or tables. Up above, it's the colorful spheres that draw the eye and complete the futuristic feeling. "They create the illusion of floating balls, which could be mistaken for Saturn," note Sebban's designers.

Inspired by the travels of Uchronia founder
Julien Sebban, Café Nuances' dreamy color
gradations are, as its designers suggest, "a veritable
ode to the gentleness of summer days."

Blue Moon Drama Makes an Entrance with a Fine Dining Experience

AGLI AMICI 1887
UDINE, ITALY
VISUAL DISPLAY

When guests walk into the new entrance and lounge of the Michelin-starred restaurant Agli Amici 1887, they are immersed in a warm, glowing blue. Indeed, as it conjures an almost immediate sense of drama, the illuminated space seems to vibrate. The idea driving this refit was to instill a sense of anticipation among diners for the gastronomic experience that awaits them inside, fully immersing them in it from the start. "The concept was born to make this space—as the first approach to the cuisine and philosophy of [Agli Amici's] chef Emanuele Scarello—a silent place suspended in time, ethereal and magical and representative of the very essence of the restaurant," says Visual Display, the designers. At the door, patrons pass through a blue curtain, which contributes to the room's theatrical feel. Once inside, the enveloping color runs from floor to ceiling, and from fabrics to furniture. The effect, the designers say, is like being "inside a precious box." Here, the dominant feature is a massive, backlit, moon-like circle on the far wall. This light installation, inspired by contemporary art, also changes color, transforming the atmosphere. Seated in comfortable blue Moroso armchairs, guests can watch Agli Amici's chefs do their thing behind their stage-like counter that's clad in a special hand-applied metallic finish. Meanwhile, they can also order cocktails prepared from a mobile blue geometric serving station that can be wheeled over to their table. Adding texture, the ceiling is also clad in a succession of sound-absorbing panels. This pattern of beams hides thin pendant lights that further sculpt Agli Amici's scintillating, experiential space.

The concept was to make this space near
silent, suspended in time. Ethereal and
majestic, the interior is representative of
the restaurant's very essence.

Out-of-This-World Cocktails
in an Otherworldly Bar

NAKED AND FAMOUS
SEVILLE, SPAIN
LUCAS Y HERNÁNDEZ-GIL / KRESTA DESIGN

If a bar was more unique and specialized, would its cocktail-drinking experience be commensurately more intense and memorable? This question inspired Lucas y Hernández-Gil's design for Naked and Famous, a trendy watering hole in Seville. Avoiding the tired tropes, the atelier created the establishment's interior, which is named after a salmon-pink mezcal-based concoction. "[It's] based on the essence of the cocktail," elucidate the bar's Spanish designers, "the mixture of different elements in a new harmonious combination." For its latest commission, the bureau thus arrived at a contrast between light and dark, color and monotone, a gesture inspired by the work of the American artists Dan Flavin, James Turrell, and Milton Avery. "Through it, we achieve an atmosphere of saturated tones where visual perception establishes connections with the sense of taste," says Lucas y Hernández-Gil. Staged inside a Sevillian patio house, Naked and Famous was conceived as a sequence of scenographic spaces. The metallic hallway off the street leads to the "Pink Room," which itself feeds into the "Laboratory Room" where the backlit bar is located. "Here we find ourselves surrounded by metalized tones and reflections, just as in a great cocktail shaker," continue the designers. And so, to accentuate this sense of juxtaposition, the "Blue Room" is also located opposite its pink sister. On the bar, acoustic foam, metal sheet, and stone wool panels provide distinctive textures, while on the floor, geometric furniture, inspired by shaped like kitchen utensils, finishes off Naked and Famous' singular, otherworldly look.

Through light and color, the designers
have created an atmosphere where
guests' can link the flavors they're encountering with what's around them.

Opposites Collide in a Dining Experience Filled with Color and Metal

FOODX
WARSAW, POLAND
LUKASZ STANIEWSKI / NOVA STUDIO

The points of departure for Lukasz Staniewski of Nova Studio's design of FoodX's fifth Polish franchise range from luxury streetwear and contemporary art to AI. Aiming to expand the size of this Warsaw restaurant while giving its interior a fresh, modern character, Staniewski also looked to the brand's signature color palette and motifs to create a space that's simultaneously minimalist and maximalist, dreamlike and futuristic. FoodX Warsaw's two levels include a dining room with a neon-pink lit mezzanine, and a new multifunctional space at basement level. Exposed brick painted in a warm beige tone provides a serene background for the brand's signature palette of neon green, mint, and stainless steel. These colors are also incorporated into furniture such as a large rounded table with an LED screen insertion in its center. These screens are present throughout the restaurant where they resemble futuristic lighting that is intended, as the designer notes, "to enrich the culinary experience with visual effects." Downstairs, mirrors, metallic fabric curtains, and steel furniture sit alongside swings—a feature it shares with FoodX's Krakow restaurant—which have been rendered in vibrant pink and fake fur. Above, an antique statue covered in graffiti dominates the space while lighting that changes color transforms the atmosphere.

Through color and neon lights, FoodX
transports guests to a futuristic
dreamscape inspired by contemporary
art, AI, and luxury streetwear.

By Day and by Night, an Explosion of Color and Light

LULU
LISBON, PORTUGAL
DC.AD

This color-intense bar, restaurant, and nightclub takes its name from the actress Louise Brooks. In 1929, Brooks played Lulu in the German silent film *Pandora's Box*, a role in which she personified the artistic period of the 1920s, specifically the Art Deco style that local studio DC.AD looked to for their Lisbon client's distinctive ambiance. The result is elegant and stylish yet contemporary, with DC.AD lending its own spin for a design that balances nostalgia with now—and wow! The space is set inside an early 19th-century building. Around every corner, Lulu is adorned with bright and bold pinks, dark greens, and whites, colors that match the similar-yet-muted tones of the building's facade. By day, the vibe is confectionary. By night, Lulu conjures a world full of other possibilities. Indeed, this quality is enhanced by its magical interior. The front room is all white—including lacquered wooden slats—with swaths of pink behind the bar, lilac on the stools, and green on the frames of tall, arched, shop-style windows. This aesthetic also extends along a mirrored wall, where an L-shaped black leather sofa lines the corner. Elsewhere, geometric patterned floors lead into the second room, where a black open space accommodates dancing, while another sinuous black leather sofa offers revelers the chance to rest and talk. Colored neon lights that line the walls and mirrors also help transform Lulu's ambiance as it transitions from day to night. A graphic sign emblazoned with the restaurant/club's name brightens up the bar. And the bathrooms, bathed in colorful lights, continue this fun, stylish feeling.

Through color and creative
lighting, this vibrant cocktail bar
offers a range of drinks and moods
depending on the time of day.

Late Nineties Nostalgia Vibrating with Color and Atmosphere

MÁLÀ PROJECT
NEW YORK CITY, NEW YORK, USA
LOVEISENOUGH

MáLà Project, a Chinese restaurant located in New York, aims to spread joy through its innovative approach to neo-Sichuanese cuisine. Based in Brooklyn's Greenpoint neighborhood, the founders came to local design studio Loveisenough with a desire to refresh and redefine their brand's visual language. Motivated by the desire to create an immersive environment within the restaurant, Loveisenough atelier's chief, Loren Daye, suggests that the commission was inspired by the cool girls of 1990s Beijing, night markets, and nature. "Overall, the concept for MáLà Greenpoint was rooted in an appreciation for a type of dining culture that we think there is a communal nostalgia for, and general feeling of comfort around," she notes. The ground floor space, inspired by the Hong Kong director Wong Kar-wai's 2004 film

2046, is a feast of color, energy, texture, and surprise. On the restaurant's red facade, neon bulbs cast light inside. Meanwhile, diners seated in the front room are treated to mint-green and red-checkered floors; walls lined in wood laminate and cherry-red vinyl panels; gold mirrors; hand-illustrated light boxes at the bar, and a metallic gold, peach, and red cloudscape on the ceiling. Down, through a neon-lit purple and lavender hall, visitors can also find a backroom decorated in green. Here, wooden vintage school chairs, a MáLà Project tradition, sit atop glossy emerald flooring. In turn, this color travels up the wall, turning from dark to light, and expanding onto the mosaic-tiled fountain filled with flowers. Lanterns with vintage textile patterns hang above, too, completing the serene ambiance.

While MáLà Project's back room is green (opposite),
nearly every element of its front room is cherry red,
including its checkered floors, vinyl wall panels,
and the metallic cloudscape on its ceiling (above).

A Cinematic Breakfast Café That Transports Visitors to Sunnier Climes

CAFÉ BANACADO
STOCKHOLM, SWEDEN
ASKA

Café Banacado's cinematic interior in Stockholm offers an escape from the everyday. Awash in pale yellow hues, the sunny ground-floor café feels warm and sweet—like the all-day breakfast it serves. Inspired by Cuba and Wes Anderson, studio ASKA, also based in Stockholm, used color, lighting, and symmetrical spatial design to create a dreamlike aesthetic. They achieved this through a yellow-and-white-checkered floor, scalloped arches, and built-in shelving, which, alongside the palette, give the space a retro, hypnagogic ambiance. Lighting, including a trio of playful, striped bulbs by glass artist Ulla Gustafsson, casts a soft, pale-yellow glow resembling the effect of a sepia lens, evoking memories of an old movie and a "time stands still" vibe. The café's cream color scheme is also present in the stainless steel bar, which is topped with yellow terrazzo. On the floor, table surfaces made of ochre tiles and light-yellow grout harmonize with the checkered pattern below. Mixed with some secondhand finds, the furnishings were custom made, with cubbyholes and shelves thoughtfully stocked with vintage LPs, potted plants, and books. Distributed throughout the space, impressionistic motifs by painter Carl Palme enhance this poetic, fantastic atmosphere.

Built-in shelves and cubby holes are
artfully stocked with vintage LPs, books,
potted plants, and secondhand finds,
giving this sunny café a retro touch.

ESPRESSO
AMERICANO
TE
CAPPUCCINO
MACCIATO
LATTE

COLD PRESSED JUICE
IMMUNEBOOSTING SHOT

SUPERFOOD LATTES
MATCHA AND LAVENDEL
BLUE MAJIK SPIRULINA

KOMBUCHA
COCONUT WATER

SUPERFOOD SOFT SERVE

Past Meets Future in an Update of a Classic Greek Restaurant

EGEO
VALENCIA, SPAIN
MASQUESPACIO

The drips of bold blue in Egeo's otherwise all-white and wood-accented space feel like they were applied by paintbrush. In reality, however, the deconstructed blue columns in this Greek restaurant based in Valencia were produced in an entirely 21st-century manner: by 3D printer. Indeed, even the columns themselves, which are split in the middle with LED tubes placed in the openings, betray an influence of technology. "We asked ourselves, 'How do we modernize this traditional Greek architectural element found in restaurants around the world?'" says Christophe Penasse, cofounder of Masquespacio, the atelier behind Egeo's interior. The challenge Penasse's team faced, therefore, was to respect the existing minimalist Greek design present at the souvlaki restaurant's third franchise (the other two are in Madrid) while creating a unique experience. Choosing to maintain the site's blue-and-white color palette, Masquespacio added whitewashed cement-like material, common in antiquity, in an effort to "materialize' Greece in the space," as Penasse explains. Above built-in banquettes, wooden tabletops with blue bases, and wooden stools shaped like hourglasses and corks, the walls feature light fittings rendered in organic forms too. Positioned in the middle of the restaurant, thereby simulating the bustling environment of a Greek market, the ordering counter is also elegantly finished in bold blue and highlighted with LEDs.

Split in the middle with LED tubes, the
signature blue columns—a deconstruction
of the traditional Greek architectural
element—were produced using a 3D printer.

A Colorful, Contemporary Pierogi Bistro with a Cheeky Night Vibe

SYRENA IRENA
WARSAW, POLAND
PROJEKT PRAGA

Sophisticated yet playful, Syrena Irena, located on Warsaw's Royal Route, is a pierogi restaurant with a difference. The interior is awash with bold blue and creamy beige, the latter reminiscent of the handmade Polish dumplings the chefs produce every day. Complementing this, the classic arches and moldings of the 1950s interior are blended with whimsical, cutout-style drawings in pink and coral tones, emblazoned with free-flowing typography. The duality of Syrena Irena's aesthetic is personified by its logo: a mermaid, *syrena* being the Polish term for these fairytale creatures. Working hand in hand with the building's interior designers, Projekt Praga, branding agency Mamastudio looked to Warsaw's city crest, which features a mermaid, as well as the 1960s, for the bistro's charming and cheeky branding.

"We were influenced by the aesthetics of jazzy Warsaw of the '60s, when this part of town was a vibrant destination for night owls and barflies," says Mamastudio explaining the influence of the Polish School of Posters, a Polish postwar design movement that inspired the atelier's recent work. "There were bright neon signs, music everywhere, colorful artsy types, and a thrilling energy." Two of Syrena Irena's walls are covered in a blue wallpaper version of the English Victorian painter Herbert James Draper's *Ulysses and the Sirens* (1909). Another is covered in a mural of colorful motifs including pierogi, wine glasses, and the moon. At night, neon lights and a retro relief of Syrena Irena's logo, displayed front and center under an arched wall, dynamically alter the ambiance of the space.

The heart of this pierogi restaurant
is a mural made of colorful,
cutout-style drawings set against
a classical backdrop.

Contrasting Colors Create an Addition to Georgia's Restaurant Scene

CHICOS TBILISI
TBILISI, GEORGIA
TAMASHI STUDIO

Chicos Tbilisi only has 18 seats, yet every month it has more than 3,000 visitors. Based between Paris and the Georgian capital, Tamashi Studio conceived the restaurant while fulfilling their client's desire to make a big impact on Georgia's food scene. "The brief was to create bright, colorful, and juicy interiors that would make Chicos the most Instagrammable restaurant in Tbilisi," the design studio says. Set inside a Soviet-era Brutalist building with tall ceilings and massive windows, the establishment makes the most of its existing features while adding a palette of contrasting beige and red. "The combination of these two very contrary colors gave the space dynamism and diversity," notes the Tamashi team. The designers produced this look primarily by leaving some of the original cement walls exposed, which then contrast polished panels that feature LED lights, and which visually divide the space. Together with a rounded glass-brick wall that also functions as a light box, these LEDs create a soft, romantic glow. "The goal was to create a sense of harmonious beauty by contrasting the building's brutalist textures with new, soft, polished materials," the designers say. Toylike furniture designed by Tamashi contributes to a sense of dynamism. "Based on the brand's mission to become an 'it' place for arts, fashion, and cultural intelligentsia, we created a space for young consumers with passion and an open mind for beauty and hedonism," conclude the design team from Tbilisi.

Whether arriving for breakfast, lunch, or dinner,
Chicos Tbilisi's guests can count on a warm
welcome that's enhanced by the restaurant's tall
ceilings and toylike furniture.

A Gallery Café in Copenhagen Where the Seats Are Works of Art

CONNIE-CONNIE
COPENHAGEN, DENMARK
TABLEAU & ARI PRASETYA

Connie-Connie is the café of the international art center Copenhagen Contemporary. Located on Amager island, which was once an industrial area, the gallery is set inside the former welding hall of pioneering shipyard Burmeister & Wain. Along with its forest-green palette, soaring ceilings, and massive industrial windows, Connie-Connie's most striking features are its chairs and benches, which were conceived by 25 different artists, architects, and designers. Asked to produce their own seats, the group created utterly unique items of furniture. "Walking into the cafeteria and knowing the artists' previous work, one will notice their specific DNA in the stools, chairs, and benches," the

café's designers, studio Tableau and designer Ari Prasetya note. Each piece of furniture was created using off-cuts from the Danish wood company, Dinesen, including the small green tables designed by Tableau. Produced in collaboration with Copenhagen-based Australian designer Ari Prasetya, these tables harmonize with the green bar, a desk by the window, as well as a dining table and chairs, all of which were also designed by Prasetya. Tableau doubled up as the project's creative director, too, and curated the space's eclectic chairs. Indeed, its hard work was soon to pay off: a year after opening in 2021, Connie-Connie won Wallpaper's annual award for best café seating.

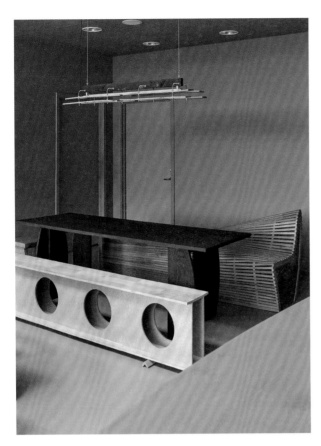

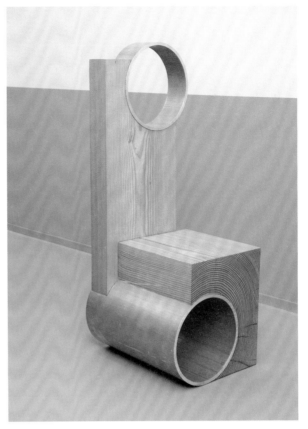

The various shapes, sizes, and
personalities of these individually
designed chairs are as diverse
as the 25 creatives who crafted them.

A 90s Italy Haven in the Heart of Montreal

CAFFETTIERA
MONTREAL, CANADA
MRDK

Located in the heart of Montreal, this layered, geometric café bar brings Italian coffee culture to North America. Inspired by the 1990s, the design reflects the owner's appreciation for Italy during that period, blending patterns, materials, colors, and vintage ephemera for a yummy effect. Faux-wood plastic laminate panels on the walls balance black-and-white-checkered mosaic floors, and colorful graphic patterns on tabletops alongside the establishment's dominant turquoise color scheme, which includes a wavy tiered element on the backlit ceiling. Curved mirrors on a wall, separated by concrete columns, reflect the image of a black terrazzo bar positioned across the room, adding depth and visual intrigue to the space. Above, a large shelf stocked with products serves as its backsplash, and on a nearby orange beam, signs, which can be adjusted depending on the time of day, indicate where to pay and order. Elsewhere, two symmetrical, tan leather banquettes are divided by a planter and flanked by hanging pendants fashioned from yellow telephone cords. Throughout the space, vintage items, including photos of '90s supermodels and Italian soccer stars, books, toys, and stickers, adorn walls and shelves. In the bathroom, this tribute to the 20th century's final decade reaches its hidden pinnacle by framing a mirror with Rubik's Cubes.

Checkered floors, geometric
tabletops, and curves contribute
to the dynamism of this layered,
1990s-inspired café.

Playful Layers and Patterns Deliver the Taste of an Italian Summer

VOLARE & BOMBOLONI'S
AMSTERDAM, NETHERLANDS
STUDIO MODIJEFSKY

The captivating interior of Volare & Bomboloni in Amsterdam West leaves a lasting impression thanks to Studio Modijefsky's intricate geometric wall patterns and their signature approach of layering elements. "The galaxy of details, textures, and colors could be overwhelming," say the designers, "but instead of competing for attention, they relax the eye as well as intriguing it." Studio Modijefsky's ambition for this Italian restaurant and cocktail bar was to create the feeling among guests that they actually might be dining in a trendy modern trattoria in Rome, Florence, or Sorrento. Complementing the tessellating shapes on the walls are vertical stripes, ceramic tiles, soft colors, rough surfaces, wood, and marble—a nod to the Italian postmodern design school of the Memphis Group in pastel tones. "Together, these details evoke white sandy beaches, colorful striped parasols blended with an easygoing vibe and the entertainment only Italians can bring to the table," says Studio Modijefsky. Wooden shelves filled with yellow backlit bottles of limoncello run around the upper perimeter of the bar, casting color on the surfaces below. Going hand in hand with the Carlo Scarpa-inspired slits and lights on the ceiling, the back bar is also constructed with layers of wood, mirrors, and marble, lending it depth. Elsewhere, these touches of optical illusion carry on in the patio, which is adorned with loose cotton fabric draping from the ceiling, giving the impression of a vast, packed space. Along with an angular chef's table, the trattoria area includes a grid of silk-screen printed posters opposite a light beige wall with mirror stripes.

Thanks to soft colors, rough surfaces,
and a sense of swagger, the space's
arches, patios, and corners conjure the
ambiance of an Italian summer.

A Dutch Chef's Debut Premises Provides a Polished and Rustic Setting

GITANE
AMSTERDAM, NETHERLANDS
STUDIO MODIJEFSKY

Angelo Kremmydas, one of Amsterdam's most acclaimed chefs, envisioned his debut restaurant, Gitane, as a reflection of his distinctive fusion of cultures and flavors, served without fuss. And in the end, thanks to Studio Modijefsky, his wish came true, with the local atelier delivering a design that's at once both welcoming and exciting. Guests enter the restaurant through a wooden vestibule topped by an orange neon bar sign that casts an enchanting glow. The tall interior features extensive wooden decor and furniture, with arched windows topped with stained glass and framed by walls that are designed to look weathered. Built-in wooden banquettes mix straight and curved lines and are decked with orange leather seat cushions. As everyone who

visits admits, however, it's in fact the bar that's the real showstopper. Made of gray and pink terrazzo, the surface sparkles, lending the drinks area a sculptural quality. This aesthetic is also emphasized by the neutral-toned back bar, whose reflection is visible in the antique dark-brown mirror above it, which sits alongside spherical lights and a darker terrazzo. Decorated in lava tiles, a column opposite the bar connects the ground floor to the mezzanine above. Beckoning diners up is a metal railing featuring alluringly curved shapes as well as a rattan-covered ceiling, an effect also applied to the level below. Beyond the front door, a terrace with orange awnings and a rounded bench offers opportunities to sip and savor the spectacle within.

Made of gray and pink terrazzo, Gitane's
showstopping feature is its bar. Nearby, a column
clad in lava tiles connects the restaurant's
dramatic ground floor to the mezzanine above.

Under Waves of Metal Mesh, a Port Town Appears in Kyiv

PORTO MALTESE
KYIV, UKRAINE
LOFT BURO

Porto Maltese is a restaurant in the Ukrainian capital with an aquatic aesthetic. Featuring a silvery-blue ceiling and jellyfish inspired lights, its design, conceived by local atelier Loft Buro, took its mark from the atmosphere of Mediterranean towns. "We wanted to take the visitor away from the city's hectic life for a leisurely visit, immersing them in the ambiance of a small port, with the opportunity to dive into the depths of the sea," explain the Kyivan designers. One method of achieving this is through the installation of mesh waves suspended above the tabletops. Creating an impression of the ocean, they also connect two halls that merge like "the bays of a port city," as the designers note.

Illuminated by a multitude of small lights, the space also contains columns made of ropes, as well as decorative white sails and ornamental gold-fish hanging from the ceiling. One wall is also adorned with a mural of the whale from Konrad Gesner's 16th-century encyclopedia *Historiae Animalium*, rendered in a shade of rusty brown, like that of a ship. Nearby, a communal table with a base inspired by corals and a wine cabinet with a shimmering exterior line the wall. "Here you can warm up in the company of close friends, share a delicious dinner, soak up the blueness of the waves, and emerge refreshed in anticipation of the next visit to the port," note the Loft Buro architects.

On the ceiling connecting both
hallways, waves of metal
mesh sway in smooth curves,
inviting visitors to explore.

A Coastal-Inspired Restaurant Unifying Industry and World-Class Design

RITZ-CARLTON AURA RESTAURANT
WOLFSBURG, GERMANY
HENN

While hotel dining experiences typically exude a predictable formality, the Ritz-Carlton Aura Restaurant in Wolfsburg, Germany, pleasantly defies the norm. Through subtle nuances, natural finishes, and a light color palette, it exudes a certain je ne sais quoi. Inspired by coastal landscapes, its warm interior offers a distinct contrast to its industrial setting. Located on a canal near the visitor center of the Volkswagen factory, the Aura's breakfast room and event space feature a glass-and-steel curved wall, presenting spectacular views of the nearby car manufacturing site. Inside, the German architecture studio Henn has divided the restaurant into three zones, created through subtle color differences that evoke, as the designers suggest, "the transition from sandy dunes to pebbled shorelines." In wood and light-colored upholstery, individual tables and chairs run along the facade, while a lounge area boasts a fireplace and camel-toned leather sofas. Elsewhere, there's intimate, monochromatic, alcove seating as well as curved teal banquettes that complement wall panels emblazoned with watercolor prints by Henn. Other wall finishes include gray travertine, wood, and hand-troweled plasterwork. Meanwhile, the lighting is provided by Bocci Series 73 pendants and Paul Matter Monolith table lamps, and the rugs are by Walter Knoll and Reuber Henning. "We used artisanal touches and hand detailing to create a sense of haptic luxury," adds the Henn team. The effect is an inimitable, site-specific creation unifying the thrust of industry and the thrill of luxury dining.

Clad in natural stone, three freestanding buffet
islands evoke the shape of stones rubbed
smooth by waves (above). Filigree screens give the
impression of sun-bleached dunescapes (opposite).

Chic Yet Relaxed, Refined Yet Casual, a Minimalist Restaurant in Sydney

ROSA
SYDNEY, AUSTRALIA
PATTERN STUDIO

Radiating lightness and freshness, Rosa is a Mexican woodfire restaurant nestled in Sydney's Mona Vale suburb, offering delicate textures to tantalize the palate. Created by Pattern Studio, also based in the city, its resplendent all-white interior was modeled on the streets and buildings of Mexican seaside towns like Tulum. "Rosa offers diners a transportive experience," its designers note. "Tactility, vibrancy, and artistic flair are expressed throughout. Everything is carefully balanced via sumptuous minimalism." Upstairs, the restaurant's all-white finish encompasses plaster walls, painted timber floorboards, ceramic sconces, and oversized pendants. Inserted here and there, however, are pieces of furniture that complement this subtle ambiance with nuanced tones,

including blond Thonet chairs and banquette cushions in beige with lightly striped resort-style pillows. Breaking up this color scheme, bright-red chilis occasionally adorn Rosa's walls, referencing the sumptuous food being prepared in the kitchen. Around the bar, sandstone, bricks painted white, Italian tumbled stone floors, and cacti produce the sensation of being in a desert oasis. "Rosa is relaxed enough for guests to wander in after an ocean dip, yet special enough to be a place where you can treat your loved ones," says the Pattern Studio team. "It's an offering that strikes a balance between being a chic getaway and a reliable local. The fit-out doesn't take center stage; rather, it happily provides the backdrop against which many long lunches and summer evenings can unfold."

The bar's sumptuous curves and patterned floor
conjure visions of Spain. Rendered joinery
speaks to the elegant resort style of Mexican
cities such as Tulum and Oaxaca.

Coffee, Bread, and Community Are the Bedrock of This Café-Bakery

FLOURIST
VANCOUVER, CANADA
STE MARIE

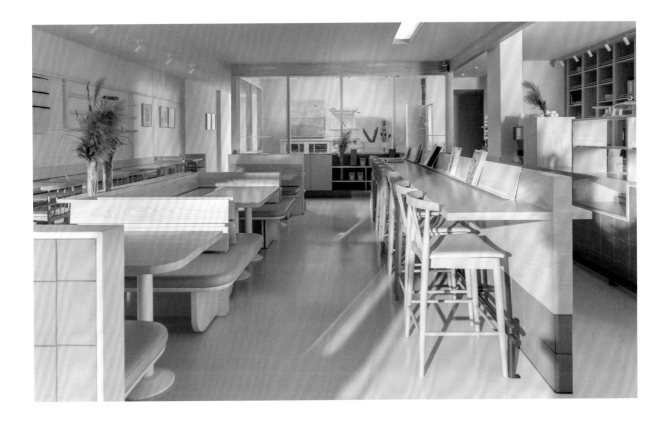

The malty tones of Flourist, a café, bakery, and community artisan flour mill near Vancouver's magnificent John Hendry Park envelops visitors as soon as they step through the door. "The emotional 'seed' of the interior is bread and sunshine," explains Ste Marie, the agency responsible for the design. Lighting further enhances these golden tones, "A counterpoint to the frequently gray skies of Vancouver," adds the Ste Marie team. From grains to beans to freshly milled flours, the provenance of everything used and sold at Flourist is 100 percent traceable. Indeed, this transparency was the building block for the design too. While conceiving the project, Ste Marie looked to the egalitarian tenets of the 18th- and 19th-century Christian Shaker communities: simplicity, utility, and honesty. "Building off of the principles and pastiche of this largely self-sufficient sect, the interior of the mill and bakery highlights abundance and warmth with a straightforward approach." Upon entry, a large table of blond stone and timber functions as a place to hold bread-making workshops. The walls are adorned with dowelled shelves, while a window is carefully embellished with Shaker-inspired jugs, tools, and vases. At the back, the working flour mill is clearly visible through glass. "A clear articulation of the transparency that informs Flourist," the designers conclude.

Flourist is a thoughtful, responsive café-
bakery whose premises were designed
to reflect the core principles of its business:
simplicity, utility, and honesty.

Function over Form in a Conscious Approach to Urban Leisure

MO DE MOVIMIENTO
MADRID, SPAIN
LUCAS MUÑOZ MUÑOZ

A scientist's lab isn't the first thing that springs to mind when thinking of Madrid's famous restaurants, but that's exactly what Mo de Movimiento looks like. Alongside its pale, cement-colored interior there are copper coils on the walls, chicken wire on the ceiling, lights fashioned from PVC electrical boxes, and massive terracotta jugs reminiscent of beehives hanging from above. On paper, it's an intimidating aesthetic, but step inside and this "experiment" starts to make sense. "It is a project with a scope on redefining the traditions and techniques of architecture, design, and consumption, within which, the creative and constructive process becomes part of the identity," explains designer Lucas Muñoz. Call it "crude refined." Muñoz has transformed Mo de Movimiento's site, based in a former theater and recording space,

into a 10,747-ft² (1,000-m²) ground-floor space for wood-fire pizza and Mediterranean dining. Designed to reimagine a more conscious kind of urban leisure, its primary stakeholder is planet Earth itself. As such, Muñoz has sought to use recycled and upcycled materials as much as possible. For instance, all of the restaurant's furniture elements, from blocky chairs to artist easel-like table bases, are reassemblies of wooden structures found at the theater before renovation. Similarly, construction debris was turned into benches, reused textiles were employed to stuff both cushions and the ceiling's acoustic panels, and the kitchen was tiled using other construction-site leftovers. Deconstructed and put back together in a new exciting form, Mo de Movimiento adds a contemporary twist to brutalist beauty.

A Harmonious Blend of Texture and Warm Materials

RESTAURANTE IDEAL
BOGOTÁ, COLOMBIA
LORENZO BOTERO ARQUITECTOS & MARTÍN MENDOZA

Adorned with familiar construction materials like red brick and sand-toned plaster, Restaurante Ideal in the Colombian metropolis of Bogotá skillfully transforms the familiar into the majestic, resulting in an inviting harmony of natural hues and unique textures that captivates visitors. On its walls and floors, artisanal brick is laid out vertically in a staggered, jointless pattern. The warm material is also accented with copper, including long linear insertions that offer a cool contrast while enhancing the material's roughness. Elsewhere on the walls, a unique beige plaster is present, created by mixing white paint and river sand. The graininess of this material adds additional texture to the hand-troweled vertical striations, which are offset by shiny accents, including large disc-shaped lights with half brass-covered bulbs. In terms of furniture and ornaments, banquettes line the walls here and there, as do potted plants in various shapes and heights. Complementing these items are paintings, a planter hugging the ceiling across from the bar, and lantern-like lamps floating from above in a lush patio space surrounded by greenery. In all, these meticulously curated features transform the quotidian into the enchanting. Around them, light filters in through fluted wood ceilings, as well as via a wall of wood-framed double windows in a cozy corner near a copper-lined fireplace.

Arranged in unconventional ways,
common construction materials such
as brick and plaster harmonize
with warm tones and unique textures.

All the Warmth of the South of France under a Kaleidoscope Dome

FOREST MARSEILLE
MARSEILLE, FRANCE
UCHRONIA

Forest Marseille embraces diners with its warm, baked-terracotta tones that evoke the sunny essence of Provence. Indeed, while this region is famous for its stunning coastline, Forest Marseille's designers from studio Uchronia in fact looked inland for inspiration, specifically to the ochre quarries of nearby Roussillon. Nevertheless, the space still retains an element of the seaside to it. For instance, the dark-orange and red lime-plastered walls are enhanced with cascading greenery as well as maritime-inspired lights, including ceramic pendants and sconces. Elsewhere, banquettes framed in olive wood line the walls, accompanied by custom-designed chairs with rust and earth-colored fabrics, alongside tables with enameled lava-stone tops in peach white. On another wall, arched blue alcoves create cozy nooks adorned with shells, coral, and intriguing objects. Inside these nooks, diners can find sculptural tabletops made of textured resin and supported by a glazed ceramic base. While the crudo bar, with its terracotta-brick base and marble surface, sets the tone as guests arrive, the bar at the back is its radiant core, where cocktails are mixed under a stained-glass dome. "Lined in a reflective metal, the round space appears like a kaleidoscope and reflects the warm tones of its surroundings," enthuses Uchronia founder Julien Sebban.

Creating a kaleidoscope of color,
Forest Marseille's stained-glass
dome (top right), located in its back bar,
is the restaurant's radiant core.

A Sensual Space That Shifts Moods Through Color and Cave-Like Spaces

BARDÓT
ANTIPAROS, GREECE
MANHATTAN PROJECTS

Deep and dark in places, yet white and bright in others, this restaurant-bar, once home to a local shipbuilding family, is infused with an ambiguous mystique, evoking the style of its namesake, Brigitte Bardot. Located on the Greek Cycladic island of Antiparos, the mood-shifting space is a seamless juxtaposition of hues and textures, traditional craft and contemporary influences, curves and straight lines, darkness and light. Guests make their way into the restaurant through a restored open-forecourt entry and a butter-yellow door. Inside, curvaceous, grotto-like spaces are coated in a white limestone wash, while a pinkish ochre casts separate areas in a dramatic tone, one enhanced by wall lighting that projects shadows and halos on the walls. Throughout this interior, quiet corners are carved into the walls with built-in seating, including an antique fireplace fashioned into a cozy daybed. Outside, however, it's all blue skies and the bright-white interior of the hemmed-in courtyard. Here, walls have been heightened and ridged by dragging a spoon-like tool across fresh stucco, creating a textured surface reminiscent of the work of the American minimalist artist Robert Ryman. In turn, these features contrast with the greenery of the surrounding nature, which includes an ancient olive tree. Indeed, the same pinkish ochre found inside is present in the built-in seating, stone tabletops, and handcrafted clay-tiled floors too. And like the smoothed-out sand and limestone floors inside, they incorporate miltos, a copper-toned mineral revered by the ancient Greeks, and likely employed by Bardót's shipbuilding predecessors.

Pink ochre connects the exterior
and interior, and is found on stone
tabletops, built-in seating, and
handcrafted clay-tiled floors alike.

In the courtyard, walls have been ridged by
dragging a spoon-like tool across fresh stucco,
producing a surface reminiscent of the work
of the American minimalist artist Robert Ryman.

A Dark, Dramatic Entrance Lights the Flame inside This Evocative Venue

ARKHÉ
NORWOOD, AUSTRALIA
STUDIO GRAM

Initial impressions are important, and Arkhé makes a big one. When you first step in, it's hard to process the sumptuousness of the lounge that awaits in this fully open-flame restaurant and bar in the Adelaide, suburb of Norwood—the first of its kind in the area. The textured lime-plastered walls in black and steel gray appear ashen and are lined with black-stained railway sleeper banquettes complete with rough finishes. Jam Factory wall lights illuminate them like embers in a fire too. "Arkhé is a bar and dining room that responds to the ritual of cooking over fire through the ephemeral nature of time and decay with an acknowledgement of the beauty in every-day life," says Arkhé's design team Studio Gram. "We took inspiration from the colors and textures of nature. There is a respect for the authenticity

of objects and materials—the imperfections are celebrated." The space is divided into clusters of distinct but harmonious spaces. A long, narrow corridor runs from the entry to the rear, establishing the entrance to the dining room and the lounge. Here, reflective polished plaster walls in warm white have been rounded, and contrast with areas of smoky black, cobbled slate floors, and sculpted service stations rendered in volcanic forms. Subtle light also filters into the space through overhead timber battens painted black, two porthole windows, and an open wall at the back, where the rear courtyard, a green oasis to retreat to, serves as a backdrop. The open kitchen, on a slightly lower level than upper-level diners, allows patrons to experience the theatrics of the open flame from above.

Through textured lime-plastered
walls in black and steel gray, the
restaurant and its open-flame grill are
filled with a sense of drama (opposite).

A Modern, Earthy Spin on Cycladic Minimalism

NŌEMA
MYKONOS, GREECE
LAMBS AND LYONS, WITH K-STUDIO

Swapping the traditional bright-white and blue colors of the Cyclades for beige and brown, Nōema on Mykonos brings a contemporary twist to Greek hospitality. This is epitomized by the restaurant's bar area, where breezeblock stands alongside raw concrete, polished cement, textured tiles, and dark wood. It is also evident in the subdued tones of charcoal, seal, and sand that embody the colors of the island, while earthenware and large plants create a tropical, Mediterranean atmosphere that reflects Nōema's natural ethos. Designed to inspire a strong sense of community and place, the restaurant, which also functions as a live music venue and concept store, is, according to its designers Lambs and Lyons (Berlin, Germany) and K-Studio (Athens, Greece), a celebration of simplicity, generosity, and spontaneity where nature rules, time stands still, and being together is what really matters. At the center of this hybrid space is a secret garden courtyard with pendant lights, a low lounge area, and lush surrounds. Although this might sound secluded, every area and feature of Nōema is intertwined with another. For instance, its open kitchen, bar, and salon radiate from this inner sanctum, creating a seamless connection as well as loosely defined areas for eating, drinking, and dancing under the sun and stars, fostering a lively and vibrant atmosphere for all to enjoy.

From plates to planters, Nōema's earthy
tones are inspired by the surrounding Greek
island of Mykonos, especially its granite
boulders, drystone walls, and golden beaches.

Natural materials, such as wood, clay, and jute,
can be found throughout the restaurant.
From floor and wall finishes to elements of decor,
the place features a satisfying mix of textures.

An Alluring Space at the Intersection of Gastronomy and Performance

AUYL
ALMATY, KAZAKHSTAN
NAAW & DUNIE

Surrounded by the powerful energy of the Medeu gorge, Auyl is an immersive restaurant whose interior is a rich amalgamation of rough textures, rich materials, exquisite ornamentation, artisan craftsmanship, lighting, and sound. According to the architects, studio Naaw, also based in the former Kazakhstani capital, the restaurant isn't just a building but embodies a full range of "emotions." Working alongside Assel Nussipkozhanova, the Milan-based Kazakh creative director of the Almaty design atelier Dunie, the two bureaus sought to produce a breathtaking, spacious, and powerful space. While the structure itself is therefore an ode to Soviet modernism that also features traditional Kazakhstani design motifs, Auyl's main stage is in fact its open kitchen. Visible from every corner of the building, including the cushioned floor seating of the tapchan area, the massive, oxidized copper domes in the ceiling above the food prep area function as a central reference for the entire restaurant. Moreover, the dining area, which offers mesmerizing views of the aforementioned Medeu gorge, is also an open space. Composed of highly textured walls and ceilings "painted a gradient from the color of pale clay to the color of dark soot," as the team from NAAW describes it, in one area linen ribbons adorned with tambour embroidery hang down in poetic waves and lines. "In general, the interior design makes use of many coarse-textured materials, including clay, undressed stone, oxidized copper, rough-hewn travertine, brushed wood and jute," explains Naaw. "This gives the restaurant's atmosphere its unique wild and primal feel."

The oxidized copper domes above the
kitchen look like bowls and visually
demarcate the guest area from the food
prep area (opposite).

A Kyivan Coffee Spot Whose Doors Are Always Open

DOT COFFEE STATION
KYIV, UKRAINE
YOD GROUP

As its massive sliding glass doors indicate, Dot Coffee Station was designed to let the city inside. Located in a vibrant area of central Kyiv, the tiny but mighty café blends a soft rhythm with urban aesthetics. "The interior is a manifestation of modern city life," says its designer Dmytro Bonesko, the cofounder of studio Yod Group. Inside, coffee drinkers are greeted by a large, pixel-like mosaic. "Every guest of Dot, like a pixel in the bright Kyiv puzzle, is the person in the big city where every day is filled with energy, emotion, and coffee," Bonesko says. Running from the wall to the floor and back up again, a narrow screen with scrolling text sets the coffee shop's rhythm. Although a popular takeaway spot, the shop's order-in furniture includes two small tables and three benches

(one in the café, one by the facade, and another in front of the stairs) made from the same old timber beams as the chunky counter. In additional sections of the interior, white mosaic tiles grace selected walls and the staircase ascending to the café, complemented by stainless steel and exposed brick, accentuating the timeless charm of the original 1900s architectural design. The effect of these gestures, explains Yod Group's chief, is part of a design strategy cultivating the impression that Dot's doors are always open. "We have opened the facade to emphasize the hospitality of the venue," Bonesko says. "In a general sense, Dot doesn't have a 'door.' Instead, we have replaced it with glass sliding doors that let the energy of the city seep through."

Dot was designed to channel the city's energy
inside its walls. And so, the surfaces are
covered with mosaic tiles featuring pixel art, thereby
mirroring the kinetic environment outside.

ВИХІД

A Kyiv Restaurant Built around the Sensual Harmony of Rough Concrete

ISTETYKA

KYIV, UKRAINE

YAKUSHA STUDIO

"With Istetyka, we focused on the essence. And to emphasize it, we created a lot of air, enhancing the power of the void," says architect and designer Victoria Yakusha, discussing how she and her team created this ethereal, pared-back Kyivan restaurant, known for its upmarket lunch options and breezy dinners. "It's minimalism but natural, sensual, and emotional," continues Yakusha. "Looking at it, you feel character, Ukrainian DNA, a living spirit." With an emphasis on materials, the space brings to life Yakusha's love of mixing and matching. And so, the rough, unpolished, tactile textures of the concrete and clay walls sit alongside the smooth finishes of wood, stainless steel, and porcelain stoneware. In other quarters, geometric shapes, such as square poufs made from

recycled plastic, are set against rounded tables as well as steel sconces that line the walls. Cold thus comes to feel warm. "It is in combining contrasts that I find harmony," Yakusha notes. At the entrance, curvy banquettes are joined by large dining tables and decor from Yakusha's very own furniture and furnishings collection, Faina. Her Ztista tables, for instance, take their name from the sustainable material where clay, recycled paper, and other natural components are applied by hand to the object's recycled-steel base. "This ancient technique known as 'valkuvannia' was used by our ancestors for building walls of a dwelling," Yakusha explains. Above them, intricately crafted macrame lamps descend, adding a final touch to Istetyka's unique ambiance and atmosphere.

Angular seating is softened by the rounded
shapes of tables and lamps. Meanwhile,
the cold concrete walls and furniture are
balanced by the warmth of clay.

Dessert in between the Rocks Inviting a Return to Nature

ZOLAISM CAFÉ
ARANYA, QINHUANGDAO, CHINA
B.L.U.E. ARCHITECTURE STUDIO

Like stumbling upon a fossil in the middle of nowhere, walking into Chinese dessert brand Zolaism's latest franchise in the Aranya district of Qinhuangdao, a coastal city east of Beijing, has the feeling of making a unique discovery. Almost disappearing into the landscape, it appears, Stonehenge-like, a few hundred meters from the Dapu Estuary which feeds into the nearby Bohai Sea. "In a seaside resort community like Aranya away from the noise of the cities, people need places to rest their bodies and spirits," suggests Zolaism's design team, B.L.U.E. Architecture Studio. "The sensual and perceptual space we've created with our intuition not only provides an environment close to nature but also inspires us to return to nature. It encourages people to put aside the burden of urban life, relax, and free their minds." Zolaism Café is situated on the north side of an old cinema. Here, facing a small open plaza, the café's frameless glass walls integrate the interior with the exterior. Under a large eave, for example, four "rocks," created with glass-fiber reinforced concrete, cast an imposing, outdoorsy presence. Seating is scattered in between them. "The plan gives the space a sense of fluidity and openness, providing guests a constantly changing experience," the designers say. Inside the two largest rocks are private relaxation rooms with built-in seating. "Zolaism reveals both the relativity, and the integration of humans and nature," the B.L.U.E. team continues. "The architectural space has become a spiritual habitat. And as a new beginning, this experiment stands as our exploration of the relationship between nature and the artificial environment."

Rocky textures contrast with frameless
glass. Through this, the dynamic play
of light and shadows changes over time,
creating the feeling of resting in nature.

144

Concrete, Rock, and Hawaiian Food Combine into This Culinary Objet D'Art

JIGI POKE
BERLIN, GERMANY
VAUST STUDIO

Jigi Poke is a Hawaiian restaurant a stone's throw away from Berlin's famous Alexanderplatz that feels chiseled—upscale caveman, even. An intimate yet imposing island of rock and stone, its designers, Vaust Studio, wanted to combine the rough with the smooth when bringing to life their client's new poke bowl dining experience. And that's exactly what they did. According to the team, what set them down this path was a 1907 photo of a Hawaiian fisherman sitting on a rock in his clothes with just his fishing gear, an image that is framed in the restaurant itself. "We appreciate the intimacy, balance, and honesty of this situation," says the team from Vaust studio, who also sought to use this opportunity to "free the concept of the poke restaurant from what is already known." Situated in old East Berlin, this rough, textured, minimalist restaurant is centered around two curvy concrete tables, where stumps of Norwegian granite and wood serve as seating. On the windows, a custom system of transparent linen curtains add drama, while boulders of varying geological formations add color and variety to the cool gray space. Separated from the seating area by a large piece of glass, the kitchen counter, where guests place their orders, blends stainless steel with rough, handcrafted concrete elements, including a chiseled rock-like element at the counter's base. At the front of the premises, a large hanging rock forms the establishment's centerpiece. Part of Jigi Poke's branding, it is nonetheless displayed like a sculpture—a fitting gesture for a restaurant design that is itself a work of art.

Amid the hustle and bustle of this intimate
Hawaiian poke restaurant are two
large concrete tables and a hanging stone,
which serves as its centerpiece.

Old Meets New in an Alpine Design Masterpiece

STEIRERECK AM POGUSCH
TURNAU, AUSTRIA
PPAG ARCHITECTS

Nestled amidst the Austrian Alps, Steirereck am Pogusch, formerly an old inn, it is the latest enterprise of the Reitbauer family, owners of Vienna's Steirereck restaurant. After decades of running this world-renowned establishment in the Austrian capital, the Reitbauers wanted to create a tangible link between the rural agricultural industry that provides Steirereck with its first-class ingredients, and the mindful way of life that stems from it. And so began this new venture. What follows is an ensemble of buildings that blends updated and elevated existing structures e.g., a 17th-century stone dwellings and a wooden house with contemporary extensions, such as two glass houses and the *Salettl* (gazebo), home to the bar and kitchen. For Steirereck am Pogusch's architects, PPAG, this latter gazebo-like structure combines with the stone and wooden structures to "form differentiated dining rooms that can serve different concepts of hospitality and atmosphere." Standing out with its cube-like facade of foamed aluminum, the *Salettl's* transparent interior opens up to the surrounding landscape through its walls of glass and its wooden-slat curtain partitions. Nearby, two angular glass houses are connected to kitchens below. Although these "large hidden worlds," as the team from PPAG describe them, feel miles away from the transparent structures above, these subterranean structures continue the contrast provided upstairs, where guests can witness the moon rise and the sun set, all from the comfort of their dining table.

The project connects several buildings, creating
an all-encompassing metabolism on the
scale of a rural settlement that serves as both
an ecosystem and an energy hub.

A Deep-down Dining Experience Like No Other

UNDER
LINDESNES, NORWAY
SNØHETTA

At Under, diners merge with the sea much like the architecture housed inside. From the outside, Europe's first underwater restaurant, Under (which means both "below" and "wonder" in Norwegian) tilts into the sea, appearing half-sunken. "In this building, you may find yourself underwater, over the seabed, between land and sea," says its designer Kjetil Trædal Thorsen, cofounder of studio Snøhetta. "This will offer you new perspectives and ways of seeing the world, both beyond and beneath the waterline." Seating up to 40 guests, Under is located in the extremities of the Norwegian coastline, at a rough, rugged, and stormy confluence where sea storms from the north and south come together. Designed with a thick concrete shell, however, the 111-foot- (34-meter-) long structure is intended to weather the elements. To this extent, its interior is calm and quiet, oblivious to any wave or wind outside, transporting diners to the beauty and mystique of the underwater world. Upon arrival, guests make their way into a hushed oak-clad foyer where glowing light from the North Sea streams up, beckoning them toward the sculptural staircase that marks their passage from land to water. Along the way down, finely woven ceiling panels in subtle colors that reference the breathtaking local sunsets accompany their tranquil journey to the dining room. From woven seats designed exclusively for the restaurant, visitors can watch the changing conditions and abundant marine life through a periscope-like window 16 feet (5 meters) below sea level. Combined with the gastronomic creations served from the kitchen, Under's unique site is sure to be one that diners will remember forever.

A Poetic, Sensory Experience That Mirrors Its Surroundings

ÄNG

HALLAND, SWEDEN

NORM ARCHITECTS

Modern and refined, Äng's interpretation of a greenhouse appears on the landscape like a solitary diamond, heralding an extraordinary sensory experience. "When it comes to haute cuisine, it's all about this interplay between the many elements that make up the experience—from architecture, design, and lighting, to taste, smell, and sounds," explain architects from Norm, the designers that created Äng. "When all these elements are balanced and well-adjusted that is when everything comes together to create a unique and esteemed experience." Set in the middle of a windswept field in one of Sweden's largest vineyards, this partially underground Michelin-starred restaurant uses craftsmanship, natural materials, and light and shadow to craft an inimitable ambiance that enhances the culinary journey. As day turns to night,

the surrounding scenery changes as well, altering the ambiance and mood of the restaurant. The interior design enhances this sensory experience with a blend of wood and stone, sculpture and ceramics, and a touch of modern Japanese design. "With the changing of light, we play on the phenomenon of chiaroscuro, a technique from visual arts used to represent light and shadow," says Jonas Bjerre-Poulsen, a founding partner of Norm Architects. "When stepping into the shadows, the vision weakens while the remaining senses intensify. One automatically pays more attention to sounds, smells, tastes, and touch and even the intuition and instinct are strengthened. This way, the surprising transition and changing of scenery prepare the guests for the next part of the holistic dinner experience."

The natural materials used to create
Äng's stunning interior, such as oak
and stone, have been refined to perfection,
making them delicate and sensuous.

ÄNG

Äng's wine cellar is a piece of art in its own
right: a deep corridor of wooden shelves
is elegant and mysterious with its subtle, soft
lighting displaying a wide selection of bottles.

A Grand Yet Intimate Island Restaurant with Monastic Feel

CROFT 3
FANMORE, UK
FARDAA

In the client's previous restaurant—operated out of their home—guests shared tables with strangers, bills were settled in the kitchen, and the client's son performed magic tricks for tips. While retaining this atmosphere, the team from London-based studio fardaa was commissioned by the owners of Croft 3 on the Isle of Mull in the Scottish Inner Hebrides to repurpose a nearby derelict basalt barn into a dining hall and restaurant. "While adapting to the grand scale of the barn and expansive landscape, the brief sought to retain the intimate and simple character of the previous restaurant," says Edward Farleigh, fardaa's founder. "Constructed from simple, raw materials, the new iteration of this beloved local restaurant feels monastic but cozy. Under its roof, the high ceiling is softened through exposed pine rafters and plywood. Together with American white ash timber floors, soft salmon-toned plaster walls, and four deep-silled windows that frame the view at seat level, they create a sense of warmth. Simple furnishings, including reclaimed French café chairs and brewers' benches painted green, enhance this effect. Made on the island from a single piece of Douglas fir, communal tables are long and narrow to encourage conversation. "The length of the tables mean that couples and small groups are commonly seated alongside people they don't know," says Farleigh, "engendering links between strangers as was the case in the previous restaurant."

Four new square windows were built into the
lower wall (opposite), providing framed views
at seating level. The tables are also long
and narrow, bringing diners closer together.

An Architect's Curry House by the Sea that Blends International Flavors

CURRY HOUSE BABBULKUND
AKASHI, JAPAN
AKIO ISSHIKI ARCHITECTS

Based in the home and workplace of its designer, Akio Isshiki, Curry House Babbulkund in Japan's southern Hyōgo region offers visitors an opportunity to enjoy dishes from Sri Lanka and India, as well as recipes closer to home. "I proceeded with the design while paying attention to the various 'mixes' surrounding the house," explains Isshiki. "[These included] usage, culture, and nationality, time and space, town and house, work and life." For this design, Isshiki blended regional materials and techniques with influences from other countries. The floor, for instance, is made of Japanese kawara tiles. Handcrafted one by one in the area, their texture and edge shape are reminiscent of the lava-stone pavements seen in Central and South America. Meanwhile, marble-pattern glazed plates were created specifically for the restaurant with images of Sri Lanka's Indian Ocean. The chairs, custom-designed for the restaurant, incorporate an attached rung that can serve as a luggage rack, providing added convenience for guests. "I aimed for a primitive design with an unknown nationality, with a simple and crude composition as much as possible," Isshiki says. Upstairs on the second floor, one side of the room features plaster mixed with red iron oxide, an attempt to "incorporate the colorful walls of each country into architecture in a Japanese context." Nearby, a large window frames the sky and the sea. "In this house, there is an air of generosity like the sea that accepts all things and leads the consciousness of those here beyond the horizon."

The plates and the chairs were specially
designed for this curry house. Alongside the
restaurant's food, the pattern and color
of the glazed dishes make for a visual feast.

A 300-Year-Old Japanese Noodle Chain Opens an Outlet in a Townhouse

KAWAMICHIYA KOSHO-AN
KYOTO, JAPAN
TD-ATELIER & ENDO SHOJIRO DESIGN

In their quest to establish a new location for their Kyoto soba noodle restaurant Kawamichiya, with a history spanning three centuries, the owners meticulously searched for premises with a rich pedigree. Luckily, that's exactly what they found via a 100-year-old townhouse located in the city's downtown area, which has now become the chain's latest outlet, Kosho-An. Designed by Kyoto-based studios td-Atelier and Endo Shojiro Design, hidden design elements that were lost in previous restorations were restored, including windows and alcoves. In doing so, they produced an interior that is at once familiar yet unusual. "Kawamichiya Kosho-An is an original townhouse that is both old and new, as well as a brand new design that fuses old and new," members of the two teams suggest. "Put simply, it is a piece of architecture imbued with

ambiguity." Here, traditional elements of the townhouse have been rejuvenated as innovative designs. For instance, the wooden doors and shoji screens have been repurposed to divide the restaurant's rooms. In terms of layout, the kitchen has become Kawamichiya Kosho-An's focal point. Placed in the middle of the design, and surrounded by views into the garden and the street outside (made possible by adjusted floor heights), it is a central node in the dining experience, connecting all elements of the restaurant. Combining rustic attributes with modern materials, the aesthetic of "old meets new" is extended through each selection. The furniture also complements this, with tabletops made from salvaged building site materials, and traditional Japanese Zabuton cushions obtained from a local shop.

Traditional Japanese materials
such as brass were blended with modern
counterparts, including lauan veneer
and OSB plywood, fusing old and new.

An Immersive Bakery Café in Red Brick and Curves

PARCONIDO BAKERY CAFÉ
GOYANG-SI, SOUTH KOREA
SUKCHULMOK

Red brick and curved walls are all around at Parconido Bakery Café in Goyang-si. Spread over three levels including a rooftop, light-colored, mosaic-cut travertine is present throughout the floors, walls, and the ceiling, shaped in waves that would be any skateboarder's dream terrain. Mixed with accents of wood and sprinkled with playful circle-shaped furniture, these minimalist areas look space age, as if gravity might give way any second, allowing you to float away. On the second level, the bakery café spreads outdoors to a large terrace in red brick, which continues up to the roof. Cut into curves and pillars with a central, trough-like silver communal table, this area is its own modern Roman Forum. According to the café's designers, Seoul-based

studio sukchulmok, the space was made to resemble European squares "where people are huddled together talking on a sunny day between red brick buildings and stone pillars." The concept, the atelier adds, was thought up by the owner, who spent his childhood in Italy and wanted to provide guests with a calming space where they can relax. Back downstairs, a wall of windows is lined with low rounded benches made of overlapping pipes covered in wood. These log-like seats emphasize the café's curves and present an ideal spot to take a break. Outside the entrance, Parconido's logo depicts a baby bird curled up comfortably in its nest. "It was built in the hope that visitors would set aside their worries in life and enjoy a relaxed mood," adds sukchulmok.

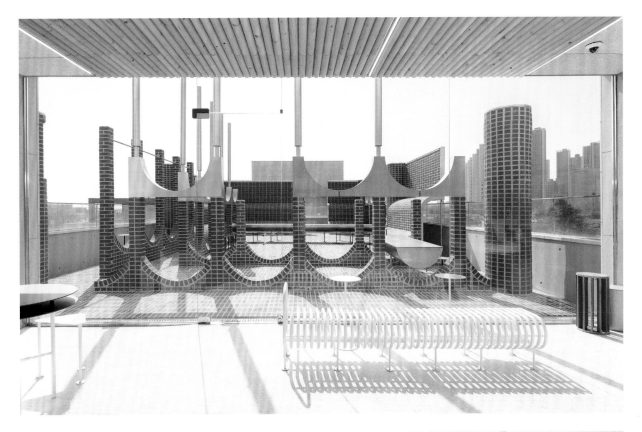

Light mosaic-cut travertine loops
around in an immersive wave
designed to envelop guests in a
nest-like feeling of calm.

The Eye-Catching Brazilian Salad Bar That Stands Out from the Crowd

OLGA RI
SÃO PAULO, BRAZIL
NITSCHE ARQUITETOS

Located on the north end of São Paulo's bustling Avenida Paulista, Olga Ri is a salad shop that demands your attention. Out front, the glass facade offers a striking view inside the lively space, where a bright-white background highlights the vibrant rainbow colors of the flooring as well as the orange staircase leading up to the second floor. Commissioned to transform the site into a physical restaurant for the previously online-only brand, local studio Nitsche Arquitetos has achieved the almost impossible feat of making the site stand out in Brazil's most populous city. The designers' goal was to create an inviting, vibrant atmosphere that exuded the company's ideals of healthy, conscious, and relaxed eating. They were also tasked with transferring the company's colorful identity, replete with geometric shapes, to the interior itself, a challenge that the team achieved with style. On the ground floor, the bright, striped mosaic floor leads guests to a welcoming area with a long stainless-steel counter where they can place their orders. Up the metal staircase, the vibrant flooring continues into the dining area, where Nitsche Arquitetos chose to preserve the building's exposed brick walls and wooden ceiling. From there, it's out onto the courtyard patio, where leafy plants cascade along the periphery, nestled within vibrant yellow bleachers and banquette seating arrangements. The vibe is playful but smart—the perfect place for a workday pick-me-up or a great destination for a casual meal with friends.

The floor is adorned with
colorful ceramic tiles
that reflect the brand's colors,
adding a vibrant touch.

A Taste of Milanese-Style Coffee Culture Arrives in Aspen

SANT AMBROEUS COFFEE BAR
ASPEN, COLORADO, USA
GIAMPIERO TAGLIAFERRI

"For their first café in the mountains, I wanted to create a unique space that would encompass both the traditional Milanese DNA of the brand as well as features inspired by Alpine style," explains designer Giampiero Tagliaferri, discussing his commission in Colorado for the Italian-American coffee-shop franchise Sant Ambroeus, based in New York City. With this in mind, Tagliaferri looked to the Alpine modernist movement for inspiration, especially figures such as Carlo Mollino, Franco Albini, and Marcel Breuer (particularly for his Brutalist approach in the village of Flaine in the French Alps). Brutalist features, including a concrete counter and curved bench, are juxtaposed with walnut, dark-green marble, faux-fur walls, and mustard-yellow corduroy seating upholstery. To enhance the coziness, the Milan-based architect incorporated Italian vintage pieces into the setting. These include Le Bambole sofas by Mario Bellini, 1950s Carlo Ratti chairs, and 1970s wall-mounted sconces. Flagstone floors contribute to the rich material palette, adding a twist of the Alps. "My hope is that the café will become a staple for Aspen locals and visitors," adds Tagliaferri. "A chic refuge where you go in the morning for your espresso and croissant, or where you stop by for a quick lunch or a delicious hot chocolate after a day on the slopes."

Troweled concrete is juxtaposed
with faux fur and Verde Alpi
marble for a warm, layered take
on Alpine modernism.

The Traditional Brasserie Reimagined through the Lens of Modern America

LAUREL BRASSERIE & BAR
SALT LAKE CITY, UTAH, USA
HOME STUDIOS

Warm and inviting, sophisticated and upscale, Laurel Brasserie & Bar's distinctive ambiance is fueled by a love for European cuisine, culture, and design. "Yet it's filtered through a decidedly American sensibility," says the restaurant's designer Oliver Haslegrave, founder of Home Studios, based in New York City. "In this commission, we sought to create that environment and treat it like an extension of the client's home, where a collection of European heirlooms and treasures have been passed down from generation to generation." On a bright-white background, Home Studios has layered marble, leather, wood paneling, and brass with opaque glass light fixtures,

reclaimed tiles, and a bold color palette that ranges from mint green to salmon. The plethora of floor finishes, ranging from checkered tile to floral-patterned carpet, alongside two stenciled walls, further accentuate this aesthetic, complemented by the presence of arched windows and doorways throughout the space. A haven for both locals and passing trade, this contemporary spin on the classic all-day brasserie is set within Salt Lake's famous Grand America Hotel in the Mountain West state of Utah. "Time-worn antiques and vintage touches from generations past all combine to make a memorable one-of-a-kind brasserie that feels fresh, vibrant, and timeless," says Haslegrave.

Layered marble, leather, wood paneling,
and brass are paired with opaque
light fixtures, reclaimed tiles, and a bold,
mint-green-to-salmon palette.

Located in Salt Lake City's Grand
America Hotel, Laurel Brasserie & Bar's
rich materials set the stage for an
experience befitting its storied setting.

An Eclectic, Layered Spot under an Umbrella of Pine Trees

LULU'S AT THE LODGE
JAMBEROO, AUSTRALIA
STUDIO BARBARA

Another vision of reality awaits visitors to Lulu's at the Lodge. "Central to our design was the desire to make guests feel at home and inspired within this hidden, mysterious, wonderful world of magic," explains Studio Barbara, the space's design team. Taking its name from the country resort and spa it is part of in the rolling hills of Jamberoo, New South Wales, this quirky, layered oasis in the pines offers visitors a unique experience. Inside Lulu's, a tiered, cake-like Murano chandelier greets guests. Immersed in a color scheme of greens, terracottas, white, and blush pinks, the interior is an eclectic mix of textures, patterns, materials, and styles, including the vibrant, geometric patterned carpet that ties it all together. The walls—striped wood battens in gradients of green, along with green-and-white painted brick—are adorned with French-hang artwork, midcentury brass wall lights, and whimsical murals on both the upper levels and ceiling. The furniture, from vintage to modern, includes customized wooden sideboards with marble fronts, floral dining chairs and low-slung vintage terracotta sofas set around a fireplace. Outside, the champagne garden is arranged around the pines. Checkerboard tabletops, scalloped white seats, and built-in seating with striped pillows pepper the abundant greenery, creating the kind of spot no one would ever want to leave. "Lulu's restaurant is intended as a space you will never forget," continues Studio Barbara. "It's a burst of energy among beautiful natural surroundings."

"Our aim was to recreate the feeling of stepping
into an eccentric holiday home somewhere in a little
French town on the coast of the Mediterranean,"
says Studio Barbara, the designers.

In the champagne garden outside, guests are
immersed in pine trees. Surrounding them, terracotta pillows with white piping, striped cushions,
and quirky tableware add depth and detail.

The Capitol Rooftop Bar Offering Presidential Elegance

LADY BIRD BAR AND ROOFTOP LOUNGE
WASHINGTON D.C., USA
MASON STUDIO

The Lady Bird Rooftop Lounge offers breathtaking views of nearly all of Washington D. C.'s most significant monuments and pays homage to one of the Capitol's most iconic and influential personalities. Named after the nickname of Claudia Alta Johnson, the wife of President Lyndon B. Johnson, Lady Bird is located atop the Kimpton Banneker Hotel and embodies the first lady's interests in the city's culture via a curated collection of art, objects, and furnishings. Throughout the rooftop, timeless natural materials, including walnut, stone, and leather, are blended with rich tones and distinctive patterns. Adjacent to the bar, a green wall with arched cutouts displaying sculptures extends into the ceiling, where shapely ceiling fans could be mistaken for patterns. Via "subtle

nods to birds' wings and patterns," as well as a mural by local artist Meg Biram, the designers from Toronto's Mason Studio have also inserted subtle references to D. C.'s official bird, the wood thrush, here and there. This aforementioned avian pattern features above the bar, which is clad in turquoise-glazed ceramic tiles. Together, these elements offer guests a relaxed, sophisticated ambiance reminiscent of Claudia Johnson's famously subtle taste. Within the bar itself, there is sculptural seating in leather, rattan, and soft blue upholstery. Outside on the terrace, custom sofas, Jardin de Ville armchairs, and seats woven from palm leaf provide a comfortable vantage point from which to appreciate the city that the real-life Lady Bird once called home.

A Celebration of Craftsmanship Nestled in Sydney's Skyline

KILN
SYDNEY, AUSTRALIA
FIONA LYNCH OFFICE

Kiln takes its name from its site, a former brickworks that was also once home to one of Australia's first clay pottery furnaces. Part of Sydney's Ace Hotel, the restaurant, based on the 18th floor, is a refined patchwork of earthy tones and materials—a celebration of Australia's craftsmanship as well as its natural environment. Featuring two restaurant areas, multiple bars, terraces, and a lounge, Kiln offers an inimitable dining experience through its unique design and decor. One of the most striking examples of this are the textiles on the walls and windows of its atrium lounge. Although they look like terrazzo, these fabrics were in fact created through a unique pigment process, where salvaged materials from the

building site were crushed into pigments and then hand-painted onto linen. Other locally sourced elements include: stone from Australian quarries; natural leather, used on banquettes and chair cushions; chunky reclaimed timber, incorporated into seating and server stations; as well as bold metal finishes, such as a brass finish on aluminum, elegantly graduated from light to dark tones. "This space is imbued with creative spirit," according to designer Fiona Lynch. "Our vision was to honor these contexts, to carry them into a contemporary interpretation through hospitality and restaurant design, and to subtly engage visitors both local and international with the rich culture outside these walls."

207

Influenced by the work of pioneering
Italian-Australian architect
Enrico Taglietti, Kiln's design also takes
its mark from Australia's nature.

A Majestic, Retro Trattoria Offering Cinematic Delights in Red

COCCODRILLO
BERLIN, GERMANY
STUDIO KIKI

Based in Weinbergspark in Berlin's central Mitte district, Coccodrillo is an Italian trattoria offering diners a taste of *la dolce vita*. Completed in 2022, Studio Kiki was commissioned by Coccodrillo's owner to whip up a dizzying, divine design in flamboyant red, one that whisks guests back to the Italy of the 1960s. An antique shade of deep red is therefore present on walls, wooden floors, velvet banquets, tables, swivel chairs, and even the curtains that adorn the floor-to-ceiling windows that wrap around the restaurant's circular terrace. "Some would compare it to Carlo Mollino's Teatro Regio," suggests Studio Kiki, referring to the Italian architect's 1967 scarlet refurbishment

of Turin's grand baroque theater. Arranged in clusters, bubble-like lights help construct a tasteful and cinematic aesthetic, which also features neon lights, murals of vintage Fiorucci posters, and mid-century modern chrome accessories. What's more, 500 space-age convex mirrors line the staircase to the bathrooms, thereby emphasizing this retro look. On the terrasse, meanwhile, guests can enjoy the comfort of 1950s-style bespoke tables and chairs, as well as flower pots that wouldn't look out of place on the Italian Riviera. As a bonus, Studio Kiki added a library room, where guests can browse nearly 5,000 vintage Italian novels. "We just adore surprises," say the designers.

Coccodrillo's flamboyant red walls, wooden floors,
velvet banquettes, spinning chairs, and long
window curtains are reminiscent of Turin's famous
baroque opera house, the Teatro Regio.

In the restaurant's library, all of its 4,900 vintage
Italian novels are flipped around. "We don't choose books
by their covers," explains Coccodrillo's design team,
Studio Kiki. "And we just adore surprises." (opposite)

Offering diners a taste of the
chicness of northern Italy,
Studio Kiki gives the Swinging
Sixties a space-age twist.

An Italian Restaurant Where Style and Opulence Meet Head-on

CARLOTTA
LONDON, UK
STUDIO KIKI

"With our restaurant, we wanted to pay tribute to the Italians who packed their bags, recipes, and heritage and took them elsewhere to create a wealth of new Italian cultures," say the owners of Carlotta, a suave, sophisticated ristorante in London's West End Marylebone neighborhood. "Whether that be a trattoria in Palermo, Sicily, or a family restaurant in New Jersey, that's what we wanted." At Carlotta, glitz and glamor don't just meet—they collide. Through a red velvet curtain, the gilded backlit bar is decked out in Rosso Levanto marble. In the dining room, supple leather banquettes with backrests that look as soft as freshly baked bread are flanked by curtained walls, gold mirrors, and family wedding photos. To top things off, the carpeted floor is an extravagant swirl of turquoise and pink. While guests are encouraged to luxuriate in the opulent menu, in the back, there's also a hidden "winners' circle" banquette for up to eight lucky diners, where, after the meal of their life, they can unwind among rose quartz wall chandeliers and artful photographs of boxing heroes—think Casablanca meets Raging Bull. Downstairs, thanks to an open kitchen, visitors have the chance to watch the chefs in action from a bank of midnight-blue suede seating. Above, a mirror-striped ceiling punctuated with a pulsating red spot reflecting the surroundings complements dining chairs in the same bold color. And don't miss the altar-style washrooms, which are, like the rest of the establishment, exquisitely fitted and decorated.

Glitz and old-school glamor are
effortlessly intertwined in this
captivating homage to Italian culture
in the heart of London.

This midnight-blue hideout, which features
a 1980s-style curved, mirrored ceilings and views into
the kitchen, will make guests forget not just the time
of day but what year it is too (opposite).

Welcoming velvet and leather furnishings in turquoise and red tones
accented by gold flourishes create an
atmosphere of luxurious elegance.

A Crimson Reverie Set in a Noble Estate in Jaipur

VILLA PALLADIO JAIPUR

JAIPUR, RAJASTHAN, INDIA

MARIE-ANNE OUDEJANS & BARBARA MIOLINI

Setting foot into the exquisite dark-red fantasy that is Villa Palladio is like stepping into a dream. Indeed, that's the idea. "The whole project began as a dream, as a mood, as a story," says Barbara Miolini, its Swiss-Italian owner. "And it slowly takes shape in all its details." While conjuring up ideas for her nine-room hotel-restaurant set in a country estate in Jaipur, northern India, Miolini called on Marie-Anne Oudejans, an award-winning, locally based Dutch designer to weave her magic as well as her intimate knowledge of European and Indian art and craft. Modeled after both the grand hotels of Italy and the legendary splendor of India's royal courts, Miolini and Oudejans also found inspiration from Jaipur's ornate buildings and impressive palette. Throughout the villa, for example, are elements in crimson, a shade that

Miolini chose as the hotel's signature in order to evoke the idea that it is "full of life, full of love." Yet, combined in various patterns and rendered in different tones, while red dominates Villa Palladio's hallways, none of its spaces are alike—including those in its restaurant. And so, while one room might share the same hue of blood orange, another will feature striped columns and flower motifs, making it feel like a vision of Venice steeped in folklore. To be sure, this aesthetic, in which certain themes seem to proliferate around a few central ideas and motifs, is also evident in the murals that adorn the property. Placed against the backdrop of Jaipur's natural beauty, the sounds and sights of Villa Palladio's garden and fountains are often set to birdsong—a fitting accompaniment for this enchanting, palatial hotel.

Villa Palladio was modeled
after both Europe's grand hotels
as well as the legendary splendor
of India's royal courts.

With each room decorated in
different patterns and colors, the hotel
proliferates with variety. Outside
are hand-painted murals by local artists.

A Colorful, Layered Celebration of Cycling and Vietnam

TIN TIN
KYIV, UKRAINE
LOFT BURO

Tin Tin isn't just a Vietnamese restaurant-bar but an ode to cycling. Upon entry, visitors are immediately confronted with bike wheels hanging artfully from the ceiling like mobiles. Move on, and you'll find wooden barstools fashioned like bike seats, and canopied booth-style sofas made to look like rickshaws. Located in the heart of Kyiv, the venue sits opposite one of Europe's oldest bike paths, built in 1913. Following the path's renovation in 2017, Tin-Tin has subsequently—and unsurprisingly—become a hotspot for the city's cyclists. Lights and transparency contribute to the space's dramaturgical quality, a feature intended to bring the street and surrounding urban environment into the interior. Before sunset, light streams in through the wall of windows where planters were placed outside to filter the sun. Afterward, the bar, made of glass cubes, lights up and casts colors on the floor. These elements are joined by tones projected by ceiling lights, which create a warm neon glow and highlight Vietnam-inspired posters and murals on the walls. Even the bathroom sparks joy. Neon backsplashes behind toilets are twisted into cheeky shapes, including a smiling dog relieving himself. Alongside this is an irreverent sign, "Time to pee pee!" What's more, the restrooms also feature optical illusion. Reflected in the mirror is a photo mural on the adjacent wall of a busy street scene full of rickshaws in Vietnam, a *trompe l'oeil* effect that the designers, loft buro, have managed to craft through Tin Tin's layered design.

Through its warm colors and abundance
of sunlight, Tin Tin transports
guests to Vietnam and its bustling
street-scene culture.

Surrounded by Nature, a Restaurant Brings the Outside In

TERRA
VYNNYKY, UKRAINE
YOD GROUP

"The space we designed mirrors its surroundings," says the team from Kyiv architecture studio Yod Group on its recent commission to create the interior for Terra, a gastronomic restaurant in the city of Vynnyky, Ukraine, just east of Lviv. Part of the Grand Emily Hotel, the establishment was designed to reflect the rolling Carpathian Mountains outside. From Terra's windows, guests can therefore watch wood fires burn in the distance at night, as well as take in the peaceful wonder of a nearby lake, which, bordered by willowy reeds on its banks, ripples in the wind. "Vast expanses, rich colors, textures and flavors, generous nature, lust for life, and existential joy. It represents the local Ukrainian vision of the four elements concept," says Yod cofounder Volodymyr Nepyivoda. Covering a generous area of 12,400 ft² (1,152 m²),

the textured space is dominated by its rounded columns, three of which are clad in Italian-made glass bricks. Lit from the inside, these supports emit a soft-green glow, while the largest one hides a wine room with the capacity for 3,500 bottles. Named after both the Latin word for "earth" and the winemaking term terroir (which denotes the complete environment in which wine is produced), Terra's wine menu is as exceptional as its food. These columns, also covered in terracotta tiles, therefore double as waiter stations, too, providing an example of innovative form and function. Another of the restaurant's most striking features is its interactive art wall. Here, guests can create patterns by moving its 2,000 copper-colored glass tiles, some of which are imprinted with images of local herbs.

The restaurant's "visual rhythm" is
created by its rounded columns. Like the
interactive wall of copper-colored glass, they
create patterns, texture, and drama.

A Lush, Welcoming World under a Canopy of Bamboo

TERTTÚLIA
GOA, INDIA
OTHERWORLDS

The heart of Terttúlia is a *balcão*, a welcoming porch commonly found in Goan homes. When design studio Otherworlds first arrived at the old Goan Portuguese-style villa where this inviting, atmospheric bar and restaurant is now established, the first thing its team noticed was that the building didn't have one of these outdoor "balconies." Motivated by "the idea of reinforcing the kinship between the house and the neighborhood," Otherworlds founder Arko Saha, suggests that the design was "conceived to grow out of the house in the form of a balcão resting under a massive bamboo canopy with an island bar central to the layout." Made of cast concrete washed in a green hue, the bar extends into built-in seating and thick organic-shaped walls and planters. Above, there's a light-green metal shelving unit with books,

bottles and arches, which mirror those of the structure's windows. When it's lit up at night like a chandelier, this feature seems to hover, as if suspended in the air. Through its elliptical openings, the immersive bamboo canopy also casts light and shadow on the ground, while green and white terrazzo ellipses scatter across the flooring, mimicking their patterns. Tall petal lights with thin stem-like bases and shades, inspired by falling leaves, are rendered in green and organic shapes nearby too. Built to accommodate the site's existing coconut trees, Terrtúlia's open, breezy space encourages chance encounters and evokes a sense of belonging. In Catalan, the restaurant's name denotes a pleasant conversation between friends, which is exactly what patrons can expect every time they visit.

Smooth Arches and European Details Create an Oasis of Calm

DAILY II

ODESSA, UKRAINE

SIVAK + PARTNERS

Daily II is a one-of-a-kind spot you want to return to again and again just to make sure it really exists. Located near the port in the old part of town, its white, curved interior was modeled after traditional Moroccan interiors, while the furniture fittings give the space a distinctly European atmosphere. "The mood there seems to be as relaxing and warm as in the traditional cafés of the old towns of Portugal, Italy, and Spain," says the team from Sivak + Partners who completed the refit in 2021. And so, beneath smooth beige arches, cane chairs and round, textured tables sit atop old wooden floorboards. Alongside them, potted plants, calmly whirling ceiling fans, and rattan panels create a warm, easygoing ambiance, offering visitors a moment of calm in their day. Although compact, the building's many rooms and alcoves nevertheless have a labyrinthine quality too. Moving from one corner to another, it's easy to become pleasantly disoriented, as if lost in a fantasy. Eventually, however, one always somehow emerges in the outside space at the back, which functions as a decentred hub. "In Odessa, there is a practice that every courtyard lives its own life and this one was no exception," note the café's designers, Sivak + Partners. The floors above Daily II's serene oasis are designated for residential use, an indication of which may also be discerned in the courtyard, where, next to tables and benches on a wooden platform, pavers demarcate the divide between public and private space. "The courtyard is like another café," continues the team from Sivak + Partners. "[It's] the same vibe, but at a much quieter pace."

As its guests move from room to room,
Daily II in Odessa provides a warm,
relaxing atmosphere that makes visitors
feel as if they're in sunnier climes.

Reviving the Great Australian Holiday Dream

BLACKSMITH PROVEDORE
LAKE MULWALA, AUSTRALIA
THE STELLA COLLECTIVE

Located on the border of the Australian states of Victoria and New South Wales, Lake Mulwala is a celebrated destination. Since the early 1960s, Australian vacationers have flocked there to spend a day out on the water soaking up the resort town's yearlong sun. Embracing that legacy, The Stella Collective from Melbourne designed Blacksmith's bar and restaurant by the lake to reflect the nostalgia of those bygone summers, introducing a new, modern sensibility that exudes subtle glamor and big dreams. At the back of the complex, where guests can paddle their boats ashore, is a bright-white modernist pavilion with a succession of dramatic arched doorways. Past the welcome mat the interior is a serene blend of soft, dry-pressed brick, sand dune walls, textured tiles, warm walnut timber, and white onyx stone. Black metal shelves, lined with wine bottles and greenery, line the wall behind the bar and the one adjacent to it, where a restored vintage Brazilian cheese cabinet serves as a centerpiece. In one corner, a roaring fireplace offers a cozy spot for guests during the winter months. Following a timber walkway outside, a rounded cabana doubles as a dance floor, while resting on the nearby grassy area are pink umbrellas in a custom tiger print. "Blacksmith draws a comparison to a Slim Aarons scene," says The Stella Collective founder Hana Hakim, referring to the late American socialite photographer. "But the design is quintessential Australiana," she continues. "The glamor and appeal of Blacksmith reminds us of the good life that exists beyond the rabbit hole. Ultimately, Blacksmith reminds us to walk on the sunny side and smile."

Black-metal accents and greenery contrast
with the serene tones of dry-pressed
brick, sand dune walls, textured tiles, warm
walnut timber, and white-onyx stone.

AKIO ISSHIKI ARCHITECTS
Japan
akioisshiki.com
Curry House Babbulkund (pp. 168–171)
Photography: Yosuke Ohtake
yosukeohtake.com

ASKA DESIGN STUDIO
Sweden
askadesignstudio.se
Café Banacado (pp. 46–49)
banacado.com
Photography: Mikael Lundblad
mikaellundblad.com

B.L.U.E. ARCHITECTURE STUDIO
China
@blue_architecturestudio
Zolaism Café (pp. 140–143)
Photography: Eiichi Kano
eiichikano.com

DC.AD
Portugal
dc-ad.com
Lulu (pp. 38–41)
@lulu.um.pub.bonito
Photography: Francisco Nogueira
francisconogueira.com
Light Design: Joana Forjaz Lighting Design
Graphic Design: Joana Areal

FARDAA
United Kingdom
fardaa.co.uk
Croft 3 (pp. 162–167)
croft3mull.co.uk
Photography: David Barbour
davidbarbour.uk

FIONA LYNCH OFFICE
Australia
fionalynch.com.au
Kiln (pp. 206–209)
kilnsydney.com
Photography: Anson Smart
ansonsmart.com

GIAMPIERO TAGLIAFERRI
United States / Italy
giampierotagliaferri.com
Sant Ambroeus Coffee Bar (pp. 186–189)
santambroeus.com
Photography: Billal Taright
billaltaright.com

GRT ARCHITECTS
United States
grtarchitects.com
Alba Accanto (p. 7)
@accantoalba
Photography: Brian Ferry
@brianwferry

HENN
Germany
henn.com
Ritz-Carlton Aura Restaurant (pp. 82–85)
ritzcarlton.com
Photography: courtesy of Autostadt
GmbH / Robert Rieger
robrie.com

HOME STUDIOS
United States
homestudios.nyc
Laurel Brasserie & Bar (pp. 190–195)
laurelslc.com
Photography: Brian Ferry
@brianwferry

**LAMBS AND LIONS,
WITH K-STUDIO**
Germany, Greece
lambsandlions.com
k-studio.gr
Nõema (pp. 116–123)
noemamykonos.com
Photography: Breba | Claus Brechenmacher
& Reiner Baumann (pp. 116, 120–121, 123)
brechenmacher-baumann.com
Photography: Robert Rieger (pp. 117–119, 122)
robrie.com

LOFT BURO
Ukraine
loftburo.com
Porto Maltese (pp. 78–81)
@portomaltese.kyiv
Photography: Serhii Polyushko
@sergey_polyushko
Tin Tin (pp. 232–237)
Photography: Andriy Bezuglov
bezuglov.ua

**LORENZO BOTERO ARQUITECTOS &
MARTÍN MENDOZA**
Colombia
lorenzoboteroarquitectos.com.co
Restaurante Idéal (pp. 98–101)
@ideal_bog
Photography: El Buen Ojo – Monica Barrenche
elbuenojo.com

LOVEISENOUGH
USA
studioloveisenough.com
MáLà Project (pp. 42–45)
malaproject.com
Photography: William Jess Laird
williamjesslaird.com
Graphic Design: Jingqi Fan
Creative Direction: Christian Castillo

LUCAS MUÑOZ MUÑOZ
Spain
lucasmunoz.com
Mo De Movimiento (pp. 94–97)
modemovimiento.com
Photography: Gonzalo Machado
@gonzalomachado

**LUCAS Y HERNÁNDEZ-GIL /
KRESTA DESIGN**
Spain
lucasyhernandezgil.com
Casaplata (pp. 14–17)
@casaplatasevilla
Photography: Juan Delgado
@mr_jdelgado
Naked and Famous (pp. 28–31)
@nakedandfamous_
Photography: Juan Delgado
@mr_jdelgado

MANHATTAN PROJECTS
USA
mpnyc.net
Bardót (pp. 106–111)
@bardot.antiparos
Photography: Yiorgos Kaplanidis
yiorgoskaplanidis.com

MARIE-ANNE OUDEJANS
India
@m.a.jaipur
Villa Palladio Jaipur
(pp. 226–231)
villa-palladio-jaipur.com
Photography: Atul Pratap Chauhan
atulpratapchauhan.com

MASON STUDIO
USA
masonstudio.com
**Lady Bird Bar and
Rooftop Lounge**
(pp. 202–205)
ladybirddc.com
Photography: Cris Molina
crismolina.com

MASQUESPACIO
Spain
masquespacio.com
EGEO (pp. 50–53)
egeosuvlakeria.com
Photography: Sebastian Erras
sebastianerras.com

MRDK
Canada
menarddworkind.com
Caffettiera (pp. 66–69)
caffettiera.ca
Photography: David Dworkind
@doubledeezy

NAAW AND DUNIE
Kazakhstan
naaw.studio
@duniedesign
Auyl (pp. 124–131)
auylrestaurant.com
Photography: Damir Otegen
(pp. 124–131)
@damir_otegen_
Photography: Yuliya Khan
(p. 131 top left)
@yulo_khan

NITSCHE ARQUITETOS
Brazil
nitsche.com.br
Olga Ri (pp. 182–185)
olgari.com.br
Photography: Arthur Duarte
arthurduarte.co

NORM ARCHITECTS
Denmark
normcph.com
ÄNG (pp. 156–161)
restaurangang.se
Photography: Jonas Bjerre-Poulsen
jonasbjerrepoulsen.com

Tasteful

New Interiors for
Restaurants and Cafés

This book was conceived, edited, and designed by gestalten.

Edited by Robert Klanten and Masha Erman

Editorial support by Effie Efthymiadi

Text by Joann Plockova
Copy-edited by Huw Nesbitt

Editorial Management by Lars Pietzschmann

Design, layout, and cover by Stefan Morgner

Photo Editor: Zoe Paterniani

Typeface: Ostia Antica by Yoann Minet and Spassky Fisher

Cover image by Joanna Pai, courtesy of Big Mamma UK (Coccodrillo, Berlin)
Back Cover image by Gonzalo Machado, courtesy of Lucas Muñoz Muñoz
(Mo de Movimiento, Madrid)

Printed by Print Best OÜ, Viljandi
Made in Europe

Published by gestalten, Berlin 2024
ISBN 978-3-96704-148-4

For more information, and to order books, please visit www.gestalten.com

Bibliographic information published by the Deutsche Nationalbibliothek.
The Deutsche Nationalbibliothek lists this publication in the Deutsche National-
bibliografie; detailed bibliographic data is available online at www.dnb.de

None of the content in this book was published in exchange for payment by
commercial parties or designers; gestalten selected all included work based
solely on its artistic merit.

This book was printed on paper certified according to the standards of the FSC®.